T0191158

My mother, Rosella Stone, served as an inspiration in
co-authoring this book because she is the backbone that
holds our family together while preserving our traditions
that have existed since before colonial contact.
—CMS

I dedicate this book, as a window or a mirror, to all
children learning about the lives of Indigenous people.
Thank you to Diane Tregarthen and Karen Ridley
for introducing me to Cheyenne M. Stone.
—GA

To the next generation of kids who can be proud to call
themselves Tongva, especially my son and niece: J & I;
and to my dad, who has consistently dedicated
his life to honoring the ancestors.
—KD

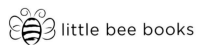
little bee books

New York, NY
Text copyright © 2024 by Cheyenne M. Stone and Glenda Armand
Illustrations copyright © 2024 by Katie Dorame
All rights reserved, including the right of reproduction in whole or in part in any form.
Manufactured in China   TPL 0624
First Edition
10 9 8 7 6 5 4 3 2 1

Library of Congress Cataloging-in-Publication Data is available upon request.
ISBN 978-1-4998-1466-8 (hardcover) | ISBN 978-1-4998-1467-5 (ebook)
littlebeebooks.com
For information about special discounts on bulk purchases,
please contact Little Bee Books at sales@littlebeebooks.com.

FSC
www.fsc.org
MIX
Paper from
responsible sources
FSC® C104723

TOYPURINA

JAPCHIVIT LEADER, MEDICINE WOMAN, TONGVA REBEL

by Cheyenne M. Stone
and Glenda Armand

illustrated by
Katie Dorame

Toypurina skipped through the woods near her village of Japchivit. She gathered shiny purple elderberries in a burden basket that she and Grandmother had made from juncus, deergrass, and sumac.

"We must think positive thoughts to create beautiful baskets," Grandmother always said.

Suddenly, the ground rolled and jerked beneath Toypurina's feet. *What is happening?* she wondered. Her heart pounding, she ran back to the village.

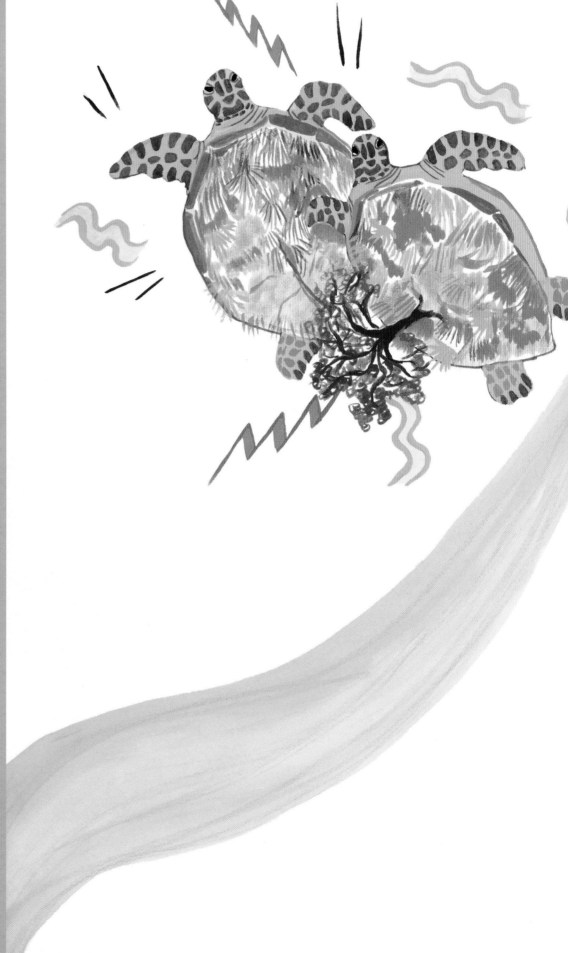

Grandmother gathered Toypurina and the other frightened children around her. Then she told them a story.

"A long time ago, the world was covered with water. Qua-o-ar, the Creator, decided to make land. Seven giant sea turtles agreed to let the Creator spread mud and grass upon their backs. The land grew. But soon the turtles began to argue. Some wanted to move east and some west. They moved in opposite directions. There was a loud snap! And the earth shook.

"And, still, from time to time," Grandmother concluded, "the turtles argue and move apart. And the earth shakes."

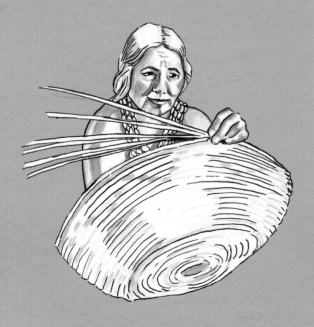

Grandmother picked up a handful of rich soil and let it fall through her fingers. "We are people of this earth. Even when the turtles cause it to move, the Creator will protect our people."

As always, Grandmother's storytelling comforted Toypurina. Soon after Mother Earth shook, Toypurina's beloved village returned to normal.

Life continued the way it had for many generations.

Just as in times past, everyone in Japchivit had a role to play. The chief protected his people and kept the peace. Medicine people had visions, performed sacred ceremonies, and healed illnesses using herbs and berries. Hunters, trappers, and fishermen provided food for the village.

Toypurina and the other children ran, swam, and played games like hoop and pole. But they also learned important skills and crafts from their parents and grandparents such as cooking, hunting, and basketmaking.

Grandmother continued passing on her knowledge to Toypurina. She taught Toypurina the art of turning the bitter acorn into nutritious food.

"Listen and observe," Grandmother said. Toypurina learned the many uses of the hard, brown fruit that fell from the giant oak. She observed how to make acorn flour, mush, and soup.

Toypurina was happy.

But one day, Toypurina, now nine years old, ran around the enormous trunk of the old oak with the other village children.

"Shake harder, Temejava!" Toypurina called to her older brother, who stood high up in the tree, shaking the branches so they could gather acorns.

Suddenly, Temejava froze. He pointed and shouted, "Look!"

Once again, Toypurina rushed to Grandmother's arms. "They have come before," Grandmother said with worry. "Why have they come back?" Toypurina asked.

As Grandmother watched the villagers accept offerings from the strange-looking men in long robes, her eyes welled with tears. "They have come to stay," said Grandmother.

Toypurina looked at the strangers and had visions of sickness and death.

Years passed, and Toypurina's visions came true. She watched in dismay as Tongva men helped the strangers build a stone village. The strangers called it Mission San Gabriel. Many of her people went to work inside the mission. But Toypurina did not want them to go.

"We are people of this earth," she reminded them, bending down and scooping up a handful of soil. "This is our land!"

Still, more and more villagers left for the mission. They became Gabrielinos, and the Gabrielinos called the strangers "padres." There were fewer and fewer people left to do the work of the village.

Those who remained in Japchivit looked to Toypurina and her brother for leadership. Temejava was named the village chief. When Toypurina was twenty-five years old, she became the medicine woman.

Toypurina used her visions and healing powers for the good of her people. She gained a reputation throughout the Tongva villages as a wise and powerful medicine woman.

Still, Toypurina had one regret. She had not stopped the devastation caused by the padres.

One morning, a Gabrielino approached Toypurina and told her about life inside Mission San Gabriel.

"At first I was happy. I learned their language. They gave me a new name, Nicolás José. But things have changed. We are no longer permitted to go between our villages and the mission. We are not allowed to speak our native tongue. Women are mistreated. We are forbidden to perform the dances and sacred ceremonies of our ancestors. Their soldiers lash us with whips and threaten us with fire-spitting sticks to make us obey."

Nicolás José's story confirmed what Toypurina had heard and witnessed over the years.

She decided she must act now. The invaders must go.

AHAAWSAKWA'AXRE

Toypurina enlisted volunteers from Japchivit, including her brother, the chief. Then she traveled to other villages, such as Jujunga and Juvit. She also visited neighboring tribes, the Chumash and Maara'yam, secretly recruiting warriors.

Many were eager to fight the invaders and reclaim their land, their traditions, and their lives. Over two dozen men joined the rebellion, even though they knew the odds were against them.

Under the crescent moon on the night of October 25, 1785, Toypurina led her warriors to the mission, bows and arrows ready. Unarmed, Toypurina carried the energy and spirit of her ancestors.

At the mission, they were met by Nicolás José. He guided the rebels into the courtyard.

"Halt!"

Guns drawn, Spanish soldiers jumped from the shadows. The soldiers surrounded the warriors. And almost before it had begun, the rebellion was over. The rebels had been betrayed by a Spanish soldier who had overheard and understood the plans of the Gabrielino rebels.

Toypurina and Nicolás José, judged to be the leaders of the attack, were put on trial. When it was her turn to testify, Toypurina stood, defiant and unflinching, before the judge. She spoke in the Tongva language.

"I came to inspire my people to fight! I asked them to listen to me and not the padres. I am angry with the padres for trespassing. I am angry that they are living here on the land of our ancestors." The padres were amazed that a woman—and one so young—spoke with such authority.

While they awaited final judgment from authorities in faraway Mexico City, the rebels remained imprisoned. After two years, their sentences were given. Nicolás José received six years of hard labor at a mission to the south. Fearing her power, the authorities gave Toypurina the harshest punishment—she was sentenced to live the rest of her life in exile, hundreds of miles away from the family, people, and land she loved.

Finally, the day came for Toypurina's sentence to be carried out. She climbed into a wagon so that Spanish soldiers could take her to the northernmost mission, San Carlos Borromeo. Her only possession was the basket she cradled on her lap.

As the wagon bumped along, Toypurina looked south toward Japchivit. She could still see the canopy of the sacred oak. The old tree had witnessed many things: her happy childhood, her lessons from Grandmother, the arrival of the padres, and her revolt.

Toypurina settled in for her long ride. It pained her to leave the people and the land she loved, but she had no regrets. Other leaders would arise. The fight would continue.

"We are people of this earth," she declared, reaching into the basket that Grandmother had made.

She held up its contents in her fist. Then she let the rich soil fall through her fingers and proclaimed,

"This is our land!"

AFTERWORD

Indigenous peoples have a rich oral tradition of preserving their culture and history. With *Toypurina*, the creators hope to add to the written history of Native Americans before and after colonial contact.

It can be said that there are only two Native American women who are widely known—Pocahontas (1596–1617), of the Powhatan tribe, and Sacagawea (1788–1812), a Shoshone. Although often romanticized, much has been written about these two remarkable women. Surely Toypurina, a brave and powerful medicine woman, deserves a place beside them in the written record.

In truth, Toypurina (1760–May 22, 1799) stands alone as the only one of these three women who fought for her own people and their way of life. The rebellion she led on the night of October 25, 1785, though unsuccessful, was an important event in Native American history. It is an example of an Indigenous people's resistance to the European presence in the Americas. That this rebellion was led by a woman makes it all the more noteworthy.

The tribe to which Toypurina belonged has been known by several names. *Tongva*, which means "people of the earth," is thought by many to be the closest to the name the early tribe members called themselves. Some call themselves the *Kizh Nation*. Others still refer to these Native Americans as *Gabrielinos* because of their association, tragic though it was, with the San Gabriel Mission. Toypurina's brother's full name was Temejavaguichia. The word in the smoke, "ahaawsakwa'axre," means "we mourn."

The purpose of the California missions and the missionaries was to convert the Indigenous people they encountered to Catholicism and claim territory for Spain. Twenty-one missions operated from 1769 until 1833.

While Toypurina was in exile, her captors arranged for her to marry a Spanish soldier. Sources say that Toypurina had been married to a Tongva man, but the padres "annulled" this marriage. Toypurina had four children. Although she died at the age of thirty-nine at Mission San Juan Bautista, the battle Toypurina began long ago continues today in a different form.

Tongva people are petitioning to have their tribe officially recognized by the federal government. They are determined to receive the rights, freedoms, and responsibilities that come with such recognition. The fight continues.

In 1542, Spaniard Juan Rodriguez Cabrillo and his crew visited the coast of present-day California. However, two centuries passed before the Spanish began to colonize California. To the elders of the tribe, the sight of the Spaniards in 1769 must have awakened memories of stories that had been passed from generation to generation.

AUTHORS' NOTES

Cheyenne M. Stone

My tribal identification is Paiute. From my paternal grandmother's side, I am Washoe. I continue both the Paiute and Washoe legacies. I was born and raised on the Big Pine Paiute Reservation in Inyo County, California. I am an enrolled member of the Big Pine Paiute of the Owens Valley, a federally recognized tribe.

I am the great-great-granddaughter of a medicine woman and, on my mother's side, a descendant of Bridgeport Tom, a medicine man. My great-grandfather, Tom Stone, was a Paiute chief, storyteller, and ethnographer. I am the granddaughter of Raymond Stone, an artist and medicine man. My father, Ross Stone, is a humble medicine man, and to this day carries on our tradition in our musa (sweat lodge).

From a young age I have attended our family's musa, learning our songs and doing my part to preserve my Paiute and Washoe lifestyle. In my mid-twenties, I began to seek knowledge of Indigenous people and their roles and lifestyles prior to colonization. I research Indigenous women who, like Toypurina, provided their people wisdom, clarity, and guidance.

When I was in fourth grade, learning about the California missions, my teacher, Ms. Duryne Willson, had the sensitivity to give me an option of making a Native American village model instead of a California mission model. In addition to sensitivity, teachers need curricula and resources to help students learn from the past and understand how all living things are intertwined with one another.

I hope this book will be a resource that will do just that. It is important to preserve stories through written text.

Glenda Armand

I live on Tongva land, near the San Gabriel Mission or Mission San Gabriel Arcángel. I have visited the mission many times, perhaps entering the very room in which Toypurina was put on trial.

Having grown up in California, I learned about the missions in school. It has been a rite of passage for fourth graders to visit a mission and make a cardboard or Styrofoam representation thereof. I did, and so did my children. As a fourth-grade teacher, I taught about the missions the way I had learned about them: from the point of view of the missionaries. The Indigenous people, who were subjected to the missionary system, were nameless and faceless.

We cannot change the past. But, henceforward, it should be *our* mission, as teachers, librarians, parents, and writers, to tell the story accurately. I hope this book contributes to that mission by introducing this remarkable woman, Toypurina, to today's children.

ILLUSTRATOR'S NOTE

Katie Dorame

Growing up in Los Angeles, I rarely read stories or saw art that represented the land and its First Peoples. I'm Tongva from my paternal grandfather's side and have been making art since I was a kid. I've always valued the books that celebrate my ancestors and their rich culture and history. There are not many of those books, even fewer are children's books, and even fewer, *if any*, are about Toypurina.

There are no photographs that exist of Toypurina or that era of the missions, so I've used many reference texts, personal photos, and my overflowing library of books that my father and I have collected over the years about all things Native California, Tongva, and early Los Angeles. I've tried my utmost to respect her legacy when reweaving things from my own imagination.

It has been an honor to illustrate these words and create something that allows this and future generations to step into Toypurina's world and learn her story. I needed this book when I was young, so I'm overjoyed to be able to read it to my child.

Selected Resources

Graham, Mary. *The Tongva: Spotlight on the American Indians of California*. New York: The Rosen Publishing Group, 2018.

Gray-Kanatiiosh, Barbara. *Gabrielino: Native Americans*. Minnesota: ABDO Publishing Co., 2004.

Hackel, Steven W. "Indian Testimony and the Mission San Gabriel Uprising of 1785." *Ethnohistory*, vol. 50 no. 4, 2003, p. 643-669. *Project MUSE* muse.jhu.edu/article/51059.

Kroeber, A. L. *Handbook of the Indians of California*. New York: Dover Publications, Inc., 1976.

Miller, Bruce W. *The Gabrielino*. Los Osos, California: Sand River Press, 1991.

Nussbaum, Ben. *California's Indian Nations*. Huntington Beach, CA: Teacher Created Materials, 2018.

Teutimes, Ernest P. Salas, Andrew Salas, Dr. Christina Swindall Martinez, Dr. Gary Stickel. *Toypurina, The Joan of Arc of California*. San Gabriel, CA: Kizh Tribal Press, 2013.

"Toypurina: California's Joan of Arc." Los Angeles Almanac. ©1998-2022 Given Place Media, Publishing as Los Angeles Almanac. 9 October 2022. http://www.laalmanac.com/history/hi710.php

Welch, Rosanne. "A Brief History of the Tongva Tribe: The Native Inhabitants of the Lands of the Puente Hills Preserve." PhD diss., Claremont Graduate University, July 2006. https://habitatauthority.org/wp-content/uploads/2013/05/native_american_history.pdf

Williams, Jack S. *The Tongva of California: The Library of Native Americans*. New York: The Rosen Publishing Group, 2003.